Literature and Cinematography

Originally published in Russian as *Literatura i kinematograf*
by Russkoe Universal'noe izdatel'stvo, 1923

Library of Congress Cataloging-in-Publication Data

Shklovskii, Viktor Borisovich, 1893-1984.
[Literatura i kinematograf. English]
Literature and cinematography / Viktor Shklovsky ; translation by
Irina Masinovsky ; introduction by Richard Sheldon.
p. cm.
ISBN-13: 978-1-56478-482-7 (alk. paper)
ISBN-10: 1-56478-482-7 (alk. paper)
1. Motion pictures--History. 2. Cinematography. 3. Formalism
(Literary analysis) 4. Motion pictures and literature. 5. Chaplin,
Charlie, 1889-1977. I. Sheldon, Richard (Richard Robert) II. Title.
PN1993.5.A1S5313 2008
778.5'2--dc22
                    2007043976

Partially funded by a grant from the National Endowment for the Arts,
a federal agency, the Illinois Arts Council, a state agency, and by the
University of Illinois at Urbana-Champaign

www.dalkeyarchive.com

Printed on permanent/durable acid-free paper
and bound in the United States of America

Literature and Cinematography
Viktor Shklovsky

translated from the Russian
by Irina Masinovsky
Introduction by Richard Sheldon

Dalkey Archive Press ▣ Champaign and London

Table of Contents

Viktor Shklovsky was the first theoretician to take a semiotic approach to the cinema. He was interested in the process by which an object shown on the screen is made to function as a sign. In Shklovsky's view, as expressed in this book, a film becomes a sign system because of the conventionality of film motion, which is being synthesized by our consciousness out of motionless photographs:

> A film does not move; it only appears to move. Pure motion, motion as such, will never be reproduced by cinematography. Cinematography can only deal with the motion-sign, the semantic motion.

What drew Viktor Shklovsky to the study of cinema? As he says in this book, a whole new medium had appeared. The temptation to study this process at its inception was irresistible. The amount of material for study was still manageable. That material could be studied and conclusions could be drawn about its nature in the scientific fashion that Shklovsky advocated. Moreover, he was eager to see whether the theories that he had developed about prose could be successfully applied to the cinema.

Shklovsky appears to have written his first piece on film in 1919[1] after his return from having served as commissar of the Russian army in Persia. In the fall of 1921, faced with arrest for his activity as a right-wing Socialist Revolutionary, he fled to Finland, and, from there, to Berlin, where he got more seriously involved in his investigation of the new medium.[2]

In Berlin, Shklovsky edited a collection of articles on Charlie Chaplin,[3] which is one of the first Soviet attempts at film analysis. As he states in his preface to that collection, he had originally intended to write a whole book comparing Chaplin's theory of comedy with the theories advanced by Aristotle and Henri Bergson. Being occupied, not to say obsessed, with his novel *Zoo, or Letters Not about Love*[4] he lacked the time for such a study. More particularly, he admitted that he lacked the technical knowledge to undertake detailed analysis of the film medium.

---

1 Viktor Shklovsky, "O kinematografe," *Iskusstvo kommuny* (23 February 1919).
2 For the context of Shklovsky's first ventures into film work, see Viktor Shklovsky, *Sentimental'noe puteshestvie* (Berlin, 1923). The English translation (*A Sentimental Journey: Memoirs*) was published by Cornell University in 1970 and by Dalkey Archive Press in 2004.
3 *Chaplin: Sbornik statei,* ed. Viktor Shklovsky (Berlin, 1923).
4 Viktor Shklovsky, *Zoo, ili pis'ma ne o liubvi* (Berlin, 1923).

Shklovsky's article in that collection—"Chaplin the Policeman"—demonstrates the truth of his admission. In the main, he confines himself to a plot summary of Chaplin's film by that name. He diffidently mentions a few qualities of the film: the use of irony, the frequent repetition of scenes and devices, the reliance on a stock character. On the whole, however, Shklovsky never really penetrates the film with his tools of analysis. Still completely dependent on tentative analogies between literature and cinema, he lacked sufficient knowledge of the medium to undertake a skillful dissection.

Shklovsky learned fast, however, as *Literature and Cinematography* shows. Here Shklovsky recognizes the cinema as a unique medium, not really analogous to literature or theater. What makes the cinema distinctive, in his view, is its total reliance on action for its effects: broad gestures, raised eyebrows, big tears, coupled with the crisp, jerky motions canonized by Chaplin. Since the action moves abruptly from one "stunt" to another—and since the stunt represents the basic unit of the action—film without plot is impossible. The plot is required to organize these units into some sort of cohesive form.

Because of the limitations imposed by what Shklovsky

then saw as the inherent nature of the medium, film strikes Shklovsky as an inferior branch of art. He explains this inferiority by recourse to the concept of continuity. According to Bergson, human thought and human movement cannot be legitimately broken into segments. Art, too, according to Shklovsky, is continuous. A poem, for example, cannot be legitimately broken into stressed and unstressed syllables, as traditional critics were wont to do.

By its very nature, however, film is discontinuous. The frames of the film move so rapidly that the eye perceives them as continuous, but unconsciously what the viewer perceives is a series of immovable objects passing before him in rapid succession. The cinema can never attain real motion, but only its simulacrum. This limitation makes the medium an extremely primitive art form, if an art form at all:

> Fundamentally, cinematography is extraneous to art. It grieves me to observe the development of cinematography. I want to believe that its triumph is temporary. A century will go by, and there will be no more dollars, marks, visas, states—but these are all trifles, details.

Not a century will go by, and human thought will overflow the limit erected in front of it by the theory of limits; humankind will learn to think in processes, and will again behold the world as continuity. Then there will be no motion pictures.

How did Shklovsky perceive the interaction between literature and the cinema? Shklovsky worried about the effect of cinema on literature. Literature could borrow from cinema such devices as the absence of motivation, the absence of psychology and the presence of staccato transitions, but Shklovsky did not recommend borrowing these devices, which he felt could lead to excessive stylization in literature.

What literature has to offer cinema is plot. In the chapter of this book entitled "Plot in Cinematography," Shklovsky discusses the ability of cinema to make use of the two main types of plot found in literature: the parallel (stepped form) and the riddle (inverted form). The former is not ideal because the cinema cannot cope with interlocking parallels and it can use a few parallels only if the same characters inhabit each one. Moreover, cinema must operate with much shorter intervals than literature and the action must usually return to the parallel at the same moment in time when it left it. For this reason, attempted rape works especially well in a film. A crime of some duration is required to permit the camera to shift to another parallel and then back again.

In most cases, Shklovsky concludes, the plot based on a riddle works better in the cinema than the plot based on a parallel. Chronological displacement can be achieved much more easily in cinema than in literature. In cinema it is simply a question of cutting a piece of film from the beginning and attaching it to the end.

The various stunts which constitute the action of the film need not be motivated. A film can show an aerial view of a city, a trained ape and a ballet in quick succession without disturbing the audience—probably because all this is shown, not told. In short, the standard film plot requires only skillful choice of scenes, chronological displacement and interesting contrasts, with the same characters all the way through to hold the scenes together. Chronological displacement has the same effect as in the novel: it creates suspense by delaying the denouement.

After analysis of the film plot, Shklovsky returns to Charlie Chaplin. In his opinion, Chaplin understands the distinctive features of the film medium perfectly and uses techniques which exploit those features to maximum advantage. His staccato motions, conventionalized and repeated in film after film, depend entirely on the propensity of cinema for exaggerated motion. Since the emphasis on motifs and action—on plot—does not permit extensive character development, Chaplin developed a stock character, instantly familiar to the audience. He plays that part in every movie against a different setting.

In his article "On the Laws of the Cinema,"[5] Shklovsky pursued his analysis of Chaplin's art further. At the bottom of Chaplin's art, Shklovsky finds the same principle of divergence that he noted in works of literature. In all his films, Chaplin, always playing the same role, creates in the audience a sensation of divergence between the constant Chaplin and the constantly changing background of each film. Shklovsky explains this divergence between Chaplin and his background as an example of narrative defamiliarization. Chaplin is always the alienated outsider, through whose viewpoint the audience interprets the society being depicted.

---

5 Victor Shklovsky "O zakonakh kino," *Russkii sovermenik,* (Cinema Laws) (1924), pp. 245-52.

Shklovsky initially did not appreciate the artistic potential of the film medium per se, but he had even less use for the color film and the "talkie." He predicted that the tendency of art to maximize conventions would prevent those new developments from ever attaining widespread popularity. Although he underestimated the viability of those developments, he never lost his appreciation of the black-and-white silent film. Several decades later, he said:

> The silent film totally excluded showy verbal conflict. In many films nowadays, the word is simply a commentary on the action. In the silent film, the spectator was in the grip of the plot, the events, from the first moments of the film. He was fascinated by the collision of feelings, which had to be expressed. In the silent, wordless film, the essence of a character could be conveyed just by a smile . . .

The silent black-and-white film was oriented to feelings. The actions required passion. Today an actor is often saved by words, music, color, painted landscapes, a wide screen. In the silent film the actor could not navigate in "shallow water," as Aleksei Tolstoy used to say. Depth of feeling was crucial.[6]

6 Mikhail Zorin, "Dialog s Viktorom Shklovskim," (Dialog with Viktor

What was it that changed Shklovsky's mind about the potential of the film medium, which in this book he sells short? Shklovsky says here that film, by its very nature, requires a plot. He believed that a plotless film, relying for its effects on repeated images, was impossible. His mind was changed by Eisenstein's film *Potemkin* (1925), which he viewed as a masterpiece.

In his article "Poetry and Prose in Cinematography,"[7] Shklovsky says that a prose work is oriented in semantics; a poetic work is oriented in form. In cinema, as in literature, when the technical elements take precedence over the semantic elements, a plotless, or poetic, film results. In *Potemkin,* Eisenstein produced such a film and showed possibilities of the medium that had not previously been imagined. For instance, Eisenstein captures the pathos of the entire revolution of 1905 in the treatment of the Odessa steps, which Shklovsky views as a prime example of the technique of *retardation.* Eisenstein builds suspense by de-

---

Shklovsky) *Lampe moei ne gasnut' . . . Literaturnye portrety, vospominaniia, razmyshleniaa* (Riga, 1976), pp. 10-14.

7 Viktor Shklovsky, "Poeziia i proza v kinematografi," (Poetry and Prose in Cinematography) *Poetika kino,* ed. Boris Eikhenbaum (Moscow-Leningrad, 1927), pp. 137-42. Reprinted in *Gamburgskii shcet* (Leningrad, 1928), pp. 160-64.

laying the denouement which cuts to the soldiers at the top of the steps and to the people at the bottom.

Shklovsky retained his commitment to the film all his life. He continued elaborating his theory of film and he wrote reviews of films. In *Hamburg Account* (1928) he spoke out against the attempts of the Party to make people write screenplays to order. He also began writing screenplays himself, producing more than two dozen over the course of his life.

In *Hamburg Account* he talks about the effect that his film work had on him:

> I have already worked in films for four years. I have worked out habits to such an extent that my head is beginning to clear and I can devote myself to literature again. Having come to films from literature, I made greater demands than the usual film person and introduced a respect for the material. In my work I do not want to develop a neutral plot against a neutral background, but to create a plot—a composition made out of the basic contradictions in the material itself. I think that this is useful for film people. Otherwise, the result is

empty frames and people on the screen with nothing to do. Yes, and this brings up a complex question—the attitude of a writer toward his time. I will now say something very naïve: in my time they demanded from film people a Soviet cinematography. Just as Napoleon ordered his chemists to invent a new sugar (not cane). I am convinced that outside art, a standing order is often useful to art. Cinematography got rid of my exclusiveness, simplified and probably modernized me. In my cinematography I see how form is created, how invention is created out of contradictions and mistakes, and how the consolidation of accidental change turns out to be newfound form. This form can exist afterward apart from the situation which created it, can even resist that situation and preserve the distinct material contained within it. The crossing of artistic form with extra-literary norms is accomplished in spurts, almost by quanta.[8]

—Richard Sheldon

8 *Gamburgskii schet,* pp. 110.

Literature and Cinematography

It is usually considered obvious that every artist wants to express something, to relate something. That "something" is called the content of a work. And the method by which that "something" is expressed—words, images, verse rhythm in literature, colors and lines in a painting—is called the form of a work.

These two aspects of every work of art are recognized by almost everyone. Some people who wish art to be of direct use to mankind usually say: the most important thing about art is its content (i.e., what it says).

The so-called aesthetes, the lovers of the beautiful, say that what matters to them is "not the what but the how" (i.e., what matters is form).

Now let's try to be sensible; let's try not to get involved in this dispute; let's not bicker. Let's just look at the nature of the dispute objectively.

We're talking about works of art.

Let's begin with an analysis of music.

Music

A musical composition consists of numerous sounds which vary in pitch and timbre (i.e., of high sounds and low sounds succeeding one another). These sounds are combined into groups which have certain relation to one another. There is nothing else in a musical composition. So, what have we found in it? We have found neither form, nor content, but material and form—that is, sounds and deployment of sounds. Now there may well be some who would say that music also has content, and that this content is its mood, whether happy or sad. But there are facts which prove a musical composition in and of itself contains neither sadness nor joy; those feelings are not the essence of music and they are not essential to its creators. A famous scholar of musical theory, Hanslik, gives an example of how Bach wrote ribald verses for his psalm music, and the music worked just as well for the ribald verses as it had for the psalms. Actually, it is not unusual for religious sects to perform their *incantations* to dance tunes. Meanwhile, for such an adaptation it is necessary to overcome the traditional association of those tunes with a certain context.

This is why the philosopher Kant defined music as pure form—that is, he rejected its so-called content.

Painting

Now let us look at the so-called fine arts. The term is not precise, and it does not encompass the phenomena in their entirety. Ornamental art, clearly, depicts nothing. However, at least in European art, the fine arts usually depict the so-called outer world: paintings of labor, men, beasts. Hardly anyone would argue with us, besides which we know from the artists themselves that when they paint flowers, or grass, or a cow, they are not interested in whether that grass can be put to good use, but only in what it looks like, that is, in terms of color and line. For an artist the external world is not the content of a painting but the material for a painting. Giotto, the famous Renaissance painter, says "a painting is, above all, a combination of colored planes." The Impressionists painted things as if they saw them without comprehending, merely as colored spots. They perceived the world as if they had suddenly awakened. That's how the Russian artist, the wanderer Kramskoi, defined the effect produced on him by an Impressionist painting.

Another realist painter, Surikov, said that the "idea" for

his famous painting "Boyarynya Morozov" came to him when he saw a jackdaw on the snow. For him, this painting was, above all, "black on white." To get ahead of my story, I will just mention that "Boyarynya Morozov" is not just a realized impression of color contrast; this painting contains many heterogeneous elements—in particular, semantic elements, but semantic units used in it as material for the artistic structure.

Because of such an attitude toward "representation"[1] there exists a tendency in art to transform a representation—the so-called organic forms, that is, the drawings of a flower, of an animal, of the grass, of a ram's horn (Buryats)—into an ornament: a design that no longer represents anything. Grosse collected very interesting data concerning this phenomenon when he researched the so-called geometric ornament. All carpet designs, Persian carpet designs in particular, are the result of transforming an organic form into a form that is purely artistic.

Such transformation cannot be explained by religious

---

1 In this context the Russian word "izobrazhenie" is translated as "representation," although other meanings of it include "expression," "portrayal," "imitation," "making out"; the literal translation of the word is "image-portrayal" or "image-expression" since "obraz" means "image."

prohibition (Mohammedism avoids image-portrayal out of "fear of idolatry"), since, in all the epochs during which the Persian art of carpet-making was developing, we have carpets which depict entire scenes with people and animals and participants, and nobody is shocked by that. We have Persian miniatures on which religious prohibitions seem to have had the same effect as they had on carpets; on the other hand, we know that in Greece at a certain period the geometric style appeared without any religious prohibitions whatsoever (the Hermitage has a vase representative of that style). Geometric depiction of the human body closely resembles the representation of stylized deer on Persian carpets.

The entire history of written language can be viewed as a struggle between principles—between the ornamental and the representational.

It is curious to note, in this respect, that written language in the beginning stages of its existence—and for some peoples, up to the present day (Turks, Persians)—had a decorative quality.

The divorce of the written sign from the representation of the conventionality of writing is caused not only by its technique, but also by the stylization of the sign, where the technical conventions are but guides along the way. A letter is an ornament.

An artist holds on to representation, to the world, not in order to create the world but to use in his creative work more complex and rewarding material. The divorce from representation, the conversion of a painting into handwriting, occurs constantly throughout the history of the arts, but artists always returned to representation.

But an artist needs the world for his painting. There is a Greek anecdote about an artist who is asked to take the muslin off his painting. "I cannot do this," said the artist. "My painting actually depicts a painting draped in muslin." There are people who want to analyze a painting by going outside its borders. They speak of Picasso in terms of demons; they speak of the whole Cubist movement in terms of war; they want to solve paintings as if they were rebuses; they want to strip a painting of its form in order to see it better.

Paintings, however, are not windows into a different word—*they are things.*

Literature

According to prevailing opinion, a work of literature is divided into form and content.

Indeed, there are many who believe that a poet has a certain thought—for instance, a thought about God—and that he puts that thought into a word.

Such words may be beautiful, so we say that the form of a work, the sound-form or the image-form, is beautiful. Such is the opinion of the majority concerning form and content in art.

But, first of all, one cannot assert that every work has content, since we know that in the first stages of its development poetry possessed no definite content.

For example, the songs of the Indians in British Guiana contain only an exclamation: "hei-ya, hei-ya." Equally nonsensical are the songs of the Patagonians, Papuans, and some tribes of North America. Poetry appeared before content.

The singer's task was not to convey a certain thought in words but to construct a set of sounds *having a definite rela-*

tion to one another that would be called form. Such sounds should not be confused with the sounds in music. Those sounds have a form that is not only acoustic but also articulative: they are made by the singer's vocal organs. Perhaps in the original poem we are dealing not so much with a shout as with an articulative gesture, with the peculiar ballet of the speech organs. Such palpability of pronunciation, the "sweetness of verses on the lips," may also vary in the reception of a contemporary poem.

In search of content, we have strayed far from the study of a poem. We look at the thing created, not as if it were a work of art but an inscription, a rebus or a picture-puzzle.

This also explains why we have hardly any works on the articulative aspect of poetry and on "motor" images in general, except for non-scientific work based as it is on the self-study of the "Glossolalia" artist Andrei Bely. Yury Tynyanov's work has not yet been published. A song containing words cannot be divided into form and content.

Words in poetry are not the means of expressing a thought; the words as such express themselves and they themselves, by their own essence, determine the course of a work of art.

"In rhyme sound prevails over content," writes A. N. Veselovsky on the subject of the folk song; "it colors a parallel. The sound calls forth an echo accompanied by a mood and a word which begets a new verse. It is often not the poet but the word that is guilty of a verse." Another scholar, Rische, says: "Instead of saying that one idea evokes another, I would have said that one word evokes another. If poets were candid, they would confess that a rhyme not only failed to interfere with their creative work but, on the contrary, gave rise to their poems, serving as a support rather than an obstacle. If I might be permitted to express myself in such a way, *I would say that mind works with puns, and that memory is the art of creating puns, which ultimately lead to the idea being sought.*"

Rather often a line of a poem appears in an artist's mind in the shape of a certain sound spot, not yet crystallized into words. Words arrive at the behest of sounds.

A. Blok told me that he had observed such a phenomenon in his own work. Victor Hugo said that the hard part is not finding the rhyme but "filling the spaces between the rhymes with poetry" (i.e., connecting the "image" aspect of the poem with the already given sound aspect).

In a word, the deeper we delve into the study of verse, the more complex phenomena of form we discover.

But poems are formal throughout, and we do not have to change our methods of study. Likewise, it is not the purpose of the so-called image-aspect to illustrate or to explain.

Potebnya's idea of the image being always simpler than the concept that replaces it is completely wrong.

In Tyutchev's poem he wrote that summer lightnings "as deaf-and-dumb demons converse with each other." Why is the image of the deaf-and-dumb demons more simple or more visual than the summer lightnings themselves?

In erotic poetry one usually gives the erotic objects various "figurative" names. The "Song of Songs" is an elaborated set of such comparisons. Here we deal not so much with an image as with what I call defamiliarization, e.g. *"ostranenie"* (from the word "strange").

We live in a poor and enclosed world. We do not feel the world in which we live, just as we do not feel the clothes we wear. We fly through the world as Jules Verne's heroes fly "through the atmosphere in a cannonball." But our cannonball has no windows.

The Pythagoreans used to say that we cannot hear the music of the spheres because it plays continuously. Thus those who live by the sea do not hear the waves, but we do not even hear the words we speak. We speak the wretched language of uncompleted words. We look at each other face to face, but we do not see each other.

The world has moved outside of our vision; all that remains is the recognition of things. We do not say "hello" to each other, we say " . . . 'lo."

The entire world through which we pass, the houses which we do not notice, the chairs on which we sit, the women with whom we walk arm in arm—they all say to us " . . . 'lo."

Tolstoy wrote in his diary: "I dusted the sofa, and then couldn't remember whether I had already dusted it . . . Therefore, if I did dust it, I did it unconsciously . . . If someone conscious had seen this action, he would have been able to reconstruct it . . . And our entire life, if spent unconsciously, is as if it had never been."

Perhaps mankind got hold of reason too soon, leaping ahead with it, as a soldier steps out of formation and starts running amok.

We live as if covered with rubber. We need to restore the world for ourselves. Perhaps all the horror (not very tangible) of our present day—the Entente, the war, Russia—can be explained by the absence in us of a sensation of the world, by the absence of art. The purpose of an image is to give an object a new name. To this end, in order to make an object into a fact of broad art, it has to be extracted from the quantity of facts of life.

For this one must, first of all, set the thing in motion, as did Ivan the Terrible when he worked over little people. The thing must be ripped from the set of habitual associations. The thing must be turned over like a log in fire.

In one of his notebooks Chekhov describes how someone had been walking down a lane for fifteen years or so, reading "a wide selection of sigs" and thinking everyday "who needs a wide selection of sigs?" At last, one day someone took down the sign and turned it sideways. Then he was able to read: "a wide selection of cigars."[2]

A poet removes the sign from the thing and turns it sideways. Things rebel, they shed their old names and, with the new ones, they take on a new configuration. A poet performs a semantic shift: he snatches a concept from the set in which it is usually kept, and with the aid of a word (trope), relocates it to a different semantic set, so that we experience the novelty of the sensation one derives from locating the thing in a new set.

This is one of the means by which a palpable thing is created. In an image we have: an object—the memory of its former name, its new name, and the associations connected with the new name.

---

2 A sig is a kind of salmon. In Russian "sigs" is written in the genitive case as "сигов"; "cigars," in the genitive case, is written as "сигар."

Not every part of a work of art is created anew by the poet; he perceives a great deal in a traditional way.

In that case, traditionally perceived parts seemingly cease having a form of their own; they are no longer elevated in the same terms; instead, they serve as material for a different construct.

Pushkin, for example, had little interest in epithets (in his letter to Vyazemsky he suggested that the latter substitute one of the epithets in Pushkin's verse for "something else" [O. Brik]).

Then the work of a poet is shifted toward different aspects of his writing. Pushkin was interested mainly in the rhythmic and phonetic aspects of his works, and, occasionally, in the plots.

There is something very curious about a certain device of contemporary artistic prose. This device has been used extensively for the purpose of creating an unusual perception of things; it is a device which has not yet been described anywhere, and which I would label the "coterminous image." Its tradition in Russian literature may be traced to the following: Dostoevsky, Rozanov, Andrei Bely, Zamyatin. One also encounters this device in the Serapoin Brothers.

Its essence is in the following: a word is chosen (usually the orchestration of this word contains a repetition, or an exotic word may be chosen). Then all the other phenomena of the work are equated with it.

Dostoevsky utilized the word "filibusters" in that manner; Rozanov picked up the expression "Brandelyasy" at some trial and, afterward, used it throughout his book *The Fallen Leaves,* equating with this word all the phenomena of Russian history.

Andrey Bely noted in his memoirs about Blok ("Epopeya," Book 2) that Merezhkovsky used to wear shoes with pompons. These pompons soon turned into something that came to define Merezhkovsky's entire life. He speaks with pompons and thinks with pompons, and so on. Here we witness a sort of mechanization of the imagery device.

The de-semanticized[3] word becomes a constant parallel to the entire row of words, which are thereby stripped of their usual perception. I cannot trace the history of this device beyond the boundaries of Russian literature; I think that Dostoevsky probably borrowed the device from Dickens, who used it with great zeal.

---

3 Shklovsky uses the term "obessmyslennoe" which literally means "deprived of meaning, sense," or "made senseless."

In *Little Dorrit,* the governess Mrs. General advises her pupils always to form the words "prunes and prisms"[4] in their minds, in order to give their lips a pretty shape.

Dickens quickly makes these "prunes and prisms" stand for a certain condition of life for the Dorrits, who have become affluent.

Dickens writes about the "heaps of prunes and prisms" with which the Dorrit's life is overflowing. The conversations about lime in *Our Mutual Friend* are used in the same way. These are conversations with which the detectives at first mask their true intentions; later, they begin to employ them as a game.

I should not stray from the subject further since I hope to elaborate this thought someday.

In any case, it appears clear to me that words for a writer are anything but a necessary evil. Words are not merely a means of saying something but the very material of a work of art. Literature is made out of words and comes into being by employing the laws of the word.

Certainly a work of literature also contains a set of ideas, but these are not just ideas invested with artistic form; this is artistic form constructed of ideas as its material.

4 Shklovsky writes "peaches and prisms."

In poetry one rhyme is opposed to another; the sounds of one word are connected with the sounds of another by repetitions; thus they form the sound aspect of a poem.

In parallelism one image is opposed to another, creating the image aspect of a work of art.

In a novel one idea is opposed to another, or one group of characters to another, and this is what shapes the semantic aspect of the work.

Thus in Lev Tolstoy's *Anna Karenina* the Karenin-Vronsky group is opposed to the Kitty-Levin group. All of the above gave Tolstoy the right to declare that "he had no use for the clever darlings who fished individual thoughts out of the work" and that "if I wanted to say in a word everything that the novel wanted to express, then I would have had to write the same novel I wrote in the first place; and if the critics now understand it already, and if they can express in a topical satire the same thing I wanted to say in my novel, then I congratulate them and boldly assert that they are capable of creating things that are greater than those I myself can create."

In a work of literature, what matters is not the thought but the cohesion of thoughts: once again I turn to Tolstoy:

"cohesion itself is formed not by an idea (I think) but by something else, and if it is impossible to express the basis of this cohesion directly, it is possible indirectly with words that describe images, actions, situations."

Therefore, ideas themselves do not constitute the content of a literary work, but, in and of themselves, they represent its material, and, in their cohesion and in their interaction with other aspects of the work, they create its form.

One cannot pluck anything out of a literary work. Attempts to draw conclusions fill an artist with indignation and contempt. Pushkin has given a pure paradigm of abstract art in his *Little House in Kolomna*. It is one of those rare and curious occurrences when the work of art is filled almost entirely with a description of the device by which it is made.

Its plot is, of course, parodic throughout. As Pushkin makes abundantly clear, plot is one of the materials, since, for a writer, both the fate of the hero and the division of a work into chapters are phenomena of the same order.

Since Pushkin knew critics so well, he wanted to put them on their guard, to warn them about the comic nature of each and every conclusion in his *Little House in Kolomna:*

XXXIX

"What? Can that be all? You're joking!"
"Not really!"
"So this is where your octaves finally led!
But, why, then, did you beat your drum so freely,
Recruit your men and step right out ahead?
You picked a fitting line of march, now really!
Couldn't you find another theme, instead?
And now, I'll bet, you won't supply a moral!"
"No . . . or rather, yes, for let's not quarrel . . ."

XL

"Here is your lesson: I hardly see much sense
In trying to hire a servant without paying.
And if one's born a man, 'tis negligence
To dress up like a girl, without well weighing
That fundamental law of nature, whence
A man who hides in skirts needs time for shaving.
For bears ill suit a woman's reputation.
No more will you extract from my narration."[5]

---

5 This quotation and the following one are taken from Alexander Pushkin: *Three Comic Poems,* trans. Williaí E. Harkins.

If Pushkin had added a similar afterword to his *Evgeny Onegin,* he could have spared Russian criticism many mistakes. Undoubtedly, Pushkin regarded both *Evgeny Onegin* and *A Little House in Kolomna* as pure form. From *Evgeny Onegin* one, too, cannot draw any conclusions; this novel is parallel to *A Little House in Kolomna*; each explains and parodies the other.

For instance, the following description from *Little House* is parodic:

XVIII

In winter early they the windows covered,
But kept in summer shutters wide
Until late evening. Pale Diana hovered
Above the hut, and watched the girls inside.
(Without this sentence not a single lover
Can be depicted; thus it is prescribed!)
So evenings passed: while mother snored in sleep,
The daughter with the moon would vigil keep.

XIX

She heard the yowls of tomcats as they stalked
Across the roofs, their ladies serenading . . .

A corresponding passage can be found in *Evgeny Onegin:*

> And all the while the moon was shining
> And with its murky light defining
> Tatyana's charms and pallid air,
> Her long, unloosened braids of hair,
> And drops of tears . . . while on hassock
> Beside the tender maiden's bed,
> A kerchief on her grizzled head,
> Sat nanny in her quilted cassock;
> And all the world in silence lay
> Beneath the moon's seductive ray.[6]

What is suspicious here, in the sense of parody, is not only the traditional nature of the image, but also the usual forms such as "unloosened braids of hair," etc. To sum up all this, I think it is already possible to say that the work of art consists of material and form.

As we have already seen, material influences form and gives it direction.

A poem composed with Russian words is composed in a different way than a poem composed with Greek or Japa-

---

6 *Eugene Onegin,* trans. James E. Falen.

nese words. If a mechanic wants to replace a car part made of steal with one made of bronze or aluminum, the new part cannot be merely a copy of the old one. New material requires new form.

Strictly speaking, translation is impossible. Indeed, Edgar Allan Poe says that he chose "raven" for his work "The Raven" only because that word looked nice next to the word "Pallas."

But in translation these words must sound different, so the logic, the artistic logic, collapses. Shakespeare translated into Russian turns out longer by almost a third, a play that lasts four hours in English will last six in Russian. Thus, translating the material of one into the material of another poses almost insurmountable difficulties. Moreover, if our pronunciation of the words is different from that of the author, we can be sure that the consonances of the work will be either inaccessible or unpleasant.

Those writers who concern themselves with semantic form—for example, Dostoevsky and Tolstoy—prove to be more or less translatable. Writers who work mainly with motor imagery and with language—such as Gogol and Leskov—or with the orchestration of verse and rhythm—such as Pushkin—can never be conveyed by translation.

Thus, Dostoevsky admired the universality of Pushkin, but Pushkin will never be a universal writer, whereas Dostoevsky managed to become universal by combining a complex plot structure with philosophic substance.

At the present time, with the invention of cinematography, mankind has acquired new opportunities for creative expression.

To my horror, I have discovered abroad that in America the film industry is the third largest industry, exceeded only by metallurgy and textiles.

Quantitatively speaking, it is mainly cinematography that represents spectacle in the world. We pay little attention to films and yet such "quantity" is already beginning to turn into "quality."

Our literature, theaters, paintings are nothing but a tiny niche, a small island, in comparison to the sea of cinematography.

Meanwhile literature, and art in general, live right next to cinematography pretending not to notice it.

Films are being made by total strangers. Attempts to make films out of literature have come to naught.

Actually, worse than naught. It appeared that one could put content of any kind on a reel. It appeared that one could abstract something from literary works and put that "something" on a reel.

Adaptations appeared in Russia, too; films have been made from Tolstoy's "Father Sergius," Pushkin's "The Station Master," and even his *Little House in Kolomna.*

Here in Germany, I have recently seen the film made from Dickens's *Our Mutual Friend* (a relatively successful choice), and I've learned that soon I will see all of Ibsen on the screen.

Of course, one can hand someone a trombone and order him to "play the Kazan Cathedral," but the result is going to be either funny or offensive.

Adaptations do not benefit from the fact that someone intends to use them in order to reproduce great works of art.

If it is impossible to express a novel in words other than those in which it has been written, if it is impossible to change the sounds of a poem without changing its essence, then it is even more impossible to replace words with a gray-and-black shadow flashing on the screen.

Gas molecules collide with each other randomly. In these random collisions they sometimes come together and sometimes they suddenly eliminate one another. As a result, we have a law—the constant law "on the expansion of gases." The individual wills of creators, inventors, and schemers come together to form the law of art, which follows its own path, determined by the development and alteration of its forms. And that's not all.

There is a phenomenon in physics that I believe is called the Brownian movement.

If you pour extremely fine powder into a flask containing water and the particles appear to be suspended in air, it will soon become noticeable that the particles are vibrating. They are being subjected to billions of invisible molecular impulses, to which they are responding.

I don't know how it is in physics. I am not a physicist. But it is so in art; art is not created by a single will, a single genius. The individual creator is only a geometric locus of intersecting lines, of forces born outside himself.

Those innumerable, profoundly ignorant creators of cinematography flow, like a river, down the right path.

Yet maybe the time has come to be aware of this path— not to the end of controlling the movement engendered outside ourselves, but in order to stop futile attempts to do that which is not possible to do, and which ought not to be done.

Now psychological novels are being converted into reels; in Russia, there was talk of turning *byliny*[7] into films.

What a monstrous endeavor! The whole essence of *bylina* lies in its stylistic devices and its rhythm; anyone who has ever worked on the *bylina* or experienced it knows that.

Poetic images, being verbal, do not lend themselves to line drawing. And those special words, those unusual words with which Tolstoy painted everyday life, taking it, by means of words, out of the sphere of knowledge and into the sphere of recognition, do not lend themselves to photography. Or take Tolstoyan registration of details, the way he focuses on a minor detail in a big painting—the moist, chewing mouth, the doctor's hand holding a cigarette between the thumb and little finger, out of aversion to the sight of blood—this, too, does not lend itself to photography. Taking the representation out of its usual focus serves as that "chut-chut"[8] which makes art. There is almost nothing in a novel that can be transferred to the screen—nothing, that is, but the bare plot.

---

7 Bylina (plural byliny)—"Russian epic"; in Russian, "былина."
8 "Чуть-чуть," or "a little bit," in Russian.

There ought to be a different path for cinematography: a path involving the reproduction of pure motion, or, in primitive terms—the path of ballet.

But ballet does not work on the screen. The reason lies not in the difficulty of combining musical themes with the reel's movement—otherwise the problem would have been purely technical—no, there is a much deeper reason, which lies at the very heart of the film medium.

Bergson investigated the Zeno paradox, or rather several of his paradoxes which prove the impossibility of motion.

Let's consider one of them. A flying arrow occupies a certain space at each moment of its flight, and it cannot occupy more than a single space—therefore, it is immobile each moment of its flight; consequently it is immobile throughout the flight: thus, motion is unthinkable.

Bergson found a way out of the difficulty posed to him by Zeno by proving that we have no right to break motion into segments. Motion is continuous. In his paradox Zeno substitutes for motion the distance covered by an object in motion.

The ancient mathematicians had a good understanding of the difference between continuous and discontinuous magnitudes—for example, between sets of numbers and lines.

They considered both sets as independent. Having proved a theorem for one set of magnitudes, they considered it essential to prove the theorem again for the other.

Human motion is a continuous magnitude; human thought represents continuity as a set of impulses, a set of segments infinitely minute, minute to the point of continuity.

In the world of art, the world of continuity, the world of the continuous word, a line of verse cannot be broken into stresses; it has no stress points: it has a place where the lines of force fracture.

The traditional theory of verse emphasizes the violation of continuity by discontinuity. The continuous world is a world of vision. The discontinuous world is a world of recognition.

The cinema is a child of the discontinuous world. Human thought has created for itself a new non-intuitive world in its own image and likeness. From this perspective, the motion picture is a tremendous modern phenomenon—in its magnitude, perhaps, not third but first.

What makes film discontinuous?

As everyone knows, a movie reel consists of a series of momentary shots succeeding one another with such speed that the human eye merges them; a series of immobile elements creates the illusion of motion.

This is a demonstration of Zeno's paradox. The eye and the consciousness perceive immobility as motion but, as it turns out, not completely.

Beyond the threshold of consciousness, all the same, remains the sensation of a series of immobile objects, rapidly succeeding one another.

A film does not move; it only appears to move. Pure motion, as such, will never be reproduced in cinematography. Cinematography can only deal with the motion-sign, the semantic motion. It is not just any motion, but motion-action that constitutes the sphere of a motion picture.

The semantic motion-sign triggers our recognition; we complete it; it does not demand our attention.

Hence—the conventional mimicry, the raised eyebrows, the large tear, movements, gestures.

Fundamentally, cinematography is extraneous to art. It grieves me to observe the development of cinematography. I want to believe that its triumph is temporary. A century will go by, and there will be no more dollars, marks, visas, states—but these are all trifles, details.

No, a century will go by, and human thought will overflow the limit erected in front of it by the theory of limits; humankind will learn to think in processes, and we will again behold the world as continuity. Then there will be no motion pictures.

We see that the basis of cinematography, providing material for the creation of form, should be action.

There will never be a film of pure motion, to say nothing of a film of abstractions, as some German artists used to dream.

And the hordes of cinema posters, advertising their romantic, detective, zoological, gimmicky, masses-pleasing films, are repeating after me: "It shall never be."

The poetics of the motion picture is a poetics of pure plot. It has been driven to this by the very nature of shooting film, though world literature is headed in the same direction. Even Russian literature, the most psychological of all the world literatures, is becoming more and more plot-oriented every day. Dumas and Stevenson are becoming classics. Dostoevsky has been rediscovered—as a writer of detective novels.

Thus film, with all its limited means, is capable of competing with literature.

Here we cannot overlook another curious phenomenon of art history.

According to the law—established for the first time, as far as I know, by me—in the history of art the legacy passes not from father to son, but from uncle to nephew.

Let me open the parentheses of a prosaic metaphor—analogy. The medieval lyric is not the direct descendent of the Latin lyric: it rather descends from the collateral line—from folk poetry that existed as a parallel collateral art during the period when classical poetry flourished.

This is proven by canonization (i.e., by the elevation of a new dominant devices, devices not familiar to the old art or, rather, not recognized—rhymes, for example). The history of Greek literature, with its successive development of the epic, lyric, drama, comedy and novel, is explained not by the creation of one form of art out of another, but by the gradual canonization of ever-new types of folklore.

When the reserves of forms in the lower, non-canonized art came to an end, the history of the development of literary forms also ended. In fact, at any given moment we have not one but several lines of literature, among which one dominates. It gains the ascendancy, while the rest subside, unconscious. Pushkin's verse form was created not by Derzhavin but by a collateral line of Russian eighteenth-century lyric poetry—by Kapnist no less than by Batyushkov. The tradition of Gogolian style, with its alternation of "low" moments and "pathetic" moments, goes back directly to the magazine and newspaper literature of his time.

Nekrasov's tradition derives from the Russian vaudeville, the tradition of Aleksandr Blok derives from the gypsy ballad—via Fet and Polonsky, of course, but nonetheless from the direct perception of the paradigms peculiar to that minor art.

The tradition of Velemir Khlebnikov is murky and involved, but it can still be traced back to the much maligned and unread Shishkovites.[9]

Blessed are the lowly ones in the history of art, for theirs is the kingdom of the future. Modern art history is so pitiful precisely because it strives to present the development

9 Followers of Admiral Aleksandr S. Shishkov (1754-1841), who, in their desire to retain the Slavonic basis of the Russian language, opposed, in vain, the linguistic and stylistic reforms proposed by Nikolai M. Karamzin and his followers.

of artistic culture as successive consecration of generations of high priests, one by the other. In reality, the progeny of great people lack talent both in life and in creative work.

For Lev Tolstoy the romantics such as Lermontov, Chateaubriand, Marlinsky and even Turgenev were not teachers but enemies against whom he fought.

Tolstoy originated from the eighteenth-century teachers who by then had already been half-forgotten and abandoned.

The most brilliant prose of our times was created by V. Rozanov, who based his work on the canon of the newspaper, the letter and the diary.

The letter is renewing literature for the second time (the first writer to do this was Richardson).

In general, this is what usually happens. Having outlived the old forms, "high" art finds itself at a dead end. Everyone starts writing well, but no one is interested.

Art forms become petrified and cease to be palpable. I think that in such a period not only does the reader not know whether he ever read a certain poem or not, but the writer also cannot remember whether he ever wrote it.

By then, the elements of the non-canonized art have

already succeeded in developing new artistic devices. The pressure of the artistic atmosphere drops and the seepage of these elements begins.

To draw an analogy (not a parallel), one may note that this phenomenon resembles the succession of tribes, the invasion of barbarians, or the replacement of classes—those enjoying cultural supremacy.

Art forms "get tired." Like tribes, they fade away. The replacement of forms usually occurs in a revolutionary manner.

The motion picture is the natural heir of theater and, perhaps, of literature. It may absorb theater, though this is unlikely.

The contemporary theater is definitely drying up. Its life is ephemeral and traditional.

Theater, like any ailing organism, is undergoing the hypertrophy of its parts. The set designer has displaced the author and the actor.

Contemporary theater treats a play in the same way as publishers of fancy art books treat the accompanying text: printed type is cheaper than illustrations, besides which tradition requires that every book have text.

Traditional theater is rotten to the core. It has two options: it can resist the attempt of the motion picture to displace it, and—it can disintegrate in order to stay alive.

The modern novel originated from collections of novellas, through the process by which the unfolding novellas grew into the frame novella. At the same time appeared the "type" connecting the separate episodes.

In early novels the hero is passive and non-psychological, just as he was in the picaresque novels and in the classical adventure novel.

After a few centuries psychology made its appearance and proceeded to motivate the hero's every step. Both in Stendhal and in Tolstoy psychology is already diminished and radically defamiliarized. The required psychological analysis of the hero's feelings is provided, but the hero's actions are not governed by his feelings. He psychologizes after his action is completed.

Without touching upon a very complex issue in Dostoevsky's novels, I will turn to the present day. At the present time, the psychological novel is coming to an end.

The constructs of Andrei Bely do not contradict my assertion. Andrei Bely is not psychological; he is as euphuistic as an Elizabethan. In his novels, psychology motivates the complex pun constructs and the parallels.

The novel is now disintegrating into separate novellas. It

is quite possible that the novel of tomorrow will consist of short stories bound together by the unity of the hero.

As to the separate parts formerly integrated into a novel, all those speeches, philosophical ruminations, etc., will loosen their ties and, within the novel itself, will exist as set pieces.

The novel, created as a literary form, is now being destroyed. The dead theater continues to subsist on the capital of traditional reverence.

But the raucous Marinetti, who was not a thinker, was right when he predicted the triumph of the variety show. In a variety show every number is interesting in and of itself; besides, many of the acts are erotic, and the crosslink with eroticism, whether we like it or not, is essential to art.

In 1919–1921, in St. Petersburg, in the Iron Hall of the People's House, Sergei Radlov made a very interesting attempt to create a new play out of material taken from circus and café chantant stunts.

In the theater the plays were written in the right way; that is, just as in one of Dickens's novels—according to the troupe's resources and the availability of stunts (i.e., according to the material). The Dickensian plays, incidentally, featured a stunt that involved a fire pump with two barrels.

Thus in Shakespearean theater the words and puns of the actors did not play an auxiliary role in the portrayal of the hero's psychology: they were used for what they were—as sound, sonorous and witty material.

This is why Lev Tolstoy was right when he said that Shakespeare's jester and King Lear both speak the same language.

In Shakespeare's *Merchant of Venice* the characters themselves are amazed that even the fools on stage speak eloquently and make brilliant puns.

One must be eloquent on stage. Radlov's experiment, though performed with great talent and appreciated by the audience, is, on the whole, a failure.

It is too soon for the variety show to coalesce into new plays. In any case, we may hope that the motion picture does not pose a threat to this theater. Cinema will develop slowly and will, in good time, create its own classics.

The interaction between cinema and literature is much more complex. One can simply brush it off by saying that literature should not concern itself with film, and it would be even simpler to say that film is making literature cinematographic.

However, these two phenomena of art differ so substantially in their respective materials that the laws of influence are difficult to define. Film took plot from literature, but, in the process, the literary plot underwent profound change.

Literature can borrow from film its swiftness, its lack of psychologism and its lack of motivations for actions.

These are, for the most part, negative characteristics. Why take the stunt and the peculiarities of film motion from the motion picture and put them into literature or on stage?

Those who recommend this are creating a new pastiche.

Chaplin's dry, staccato movements, with their ready-made traditional devices—Chaplin walks, Chaplin smiles, etc.—are characteristic cinematic devices, engendered by the film just as the *bylina* was engendered by the word.

Introducing Chaplinism into literature is like making "ice-cream out of lilacs." You have to work in the material. A contemporary plot-oriented novel or novella follows a path of its own and the immense possibilities of the word.

Film draws heavily for its material on the stunt.

Plot is needed in cinematography to motivate the stunt.

My job in the second part of my work is to explain the profound changes a plot undergoes in a motion picture.

Plot in Cinematography

To do a proper study on the theory of cinematography, you would have to collect all films, or at least several thousand of them.

When classified, these films might yield the mass of material from which you could formulate several absolutely precise laws.

It's too bad that art history institutes and the academies are more interested in Atlantis and the Pamir excavations.

We witnessed the arrival of cinematography; its life is the life of our generation; we can trace it step by step.

Soon the material will become boundless. It is depressing to think that we already know everything about the need to study contemporary phenomena in the history of art but never do anything about it.

This is not something I can do by myself.

This matter is beyond the capabilities of one individual; it requires trained assistants, means and, possibly, experiments.

What makes people cry?

What is comical?

Under what conditions does the comic become tragic?

It's hard to understand literature fully; it's impossible, or nearly impossible, to give it direction.

The cinema is still visible; we could create a film science, which could be completely mechanized.

In 1917 someone published a carefully researched article which reported that screenwriters, exhausted by work, had concocted a machine that produced plots.

Imagine a row of films wound on special spools. One of the reels contains people's professions, the second one—countries of the world, the third one—various ages, the fourth one—human acts (for example, kissing, climbing a pipe, knocking someone down, jumping into the water, shooting). A person takes hold of the cranks leading to these reels and spins them.

Then he peers through a special slot and reads the resulting gibberish.

The machine is rather strange, but apparently it gives American brains the jolt they require.

I'm going to write more about this amazing aspect of cinematography: about the tendency not to motivate the connection between the component parts, its scenes.

But in order to do this, we have to go back to the subject of plot in literature. There are several types of literary plot (i.e., the plot of works written in words).

Almost always, as it seems to me, these types of structure are based on an underlying sensation of disparity, an irony of sorts that is resolved at the end. In its simplest cases, a plot may be defined as an elaborated parallel.

And there is an affinity that exists between parallelism in itself and the so-called *obraznost'*.[10]

For example, if we say of a great man that he is a "tower," that is an image.

As a parallelism, the construct would be as follows:

> Just as a tower rises amidst the city,
>
> So rises this man amongst the people.

That is, an image is like a parallelism with its first part suppressed. This may be elaborated into a plot. For instance, in the French erotic lexicon a certain erotic act performed swiftly is called "catching the sparrow."

In Boccaccio, due perhaps to the peculiarity of the Italian erotic lexicon, the same moment is described as "catching the nightingale," and is elaborated into a beautiful novella.

---

10 Obraznost' (Russian "образность") is not quite equivalent to the English "imagery"; it rather means "the quality of possessing imagery."

A young girl in love asks to be let into the garden to listen to a nightingale; she meets a young man there.

In the morning they are found together: they have "caught a nightingale." In Boccaccio all of that is much more elaborate than my summary indicates.

We have found the same motif in Batyushkov.

In erotic folklore, such elaborations are very common.

Thus in the simple types of plot we encounter a phenomenon similar in its structure to the "image" and the "pun." There is such a moment in the plot of Shakespeare's *Macbeth*. The witches have predicted that "none of woman born" will kill him. But Macbeth's adversary was not born, he was "from his mother's womb / Untimely ripp'd."

Thus the fact of unnatural childbirth—by means of Caesarian section—had so astonished the anonymous creator that he appropriated it and elaborated it into a plot.

The word "born" lies at the base of the plot construct. For Macbeth, it means "of woman born"; for the witch, it means "born naturally," with the emphasis on the very process of childbirth. Thus we find ourselves in a sphere where disparities are created on linguistic grounds.

This plot, like Boccaccio's plot, cannot be translated into

film. The plot of the "righteous judgment" is very popular in folklore.

In the Bible (to be precise, in the canonic Book of Daniel) it appears as follows.

The elders accuse Shoshana of fornicating with a certain youth, which act they have witnessed.

The wise judge questions them individually as to where and under what tree it took place. Each of the elders names a different tree.

The accusation is refuted.

The same motif is present in the numerous judgments of Solomon. In Samoan folk tales the subject is a stolen stone; the judge, in order to make a decision, asks every contender to sculpt the shape of the stone.

Thus we are talking about the most ordinary collation of testimony. These days that kind of plot is impossible.

At that time, however, such legal action had the quality of solving a riddle. Curiously enough, this device is already parodied in *A Thousand and One Nights*. In that book, two men come to the Qadi, and each claims to be owner of a certain sack.

The Qadi inquires about the contents of the sack.

Each man begins to enumerate the items. They take turns speaking and continually add to what has already been mentioned; one claims that there are thousands of camels in the sack, the other—that it contains a whole tribe of Kurds, etc. It turns out that the sack contains three orange seeds. This plot is perceived in the context of those innumerable tales about a judge able to determine the true owner of things by posing various questions.

From the perspective of history and literary theory, this is an extraordinarily curious phenomenon.

When the inner form of a subject fades, the sensation of disparity and its resolution disappears and the entire work of art is taken as parody.

But let's return to the classification of plots. As we have seen, plots come in two varieties: the plot as elaborated parallel and the plot as riddle. Studying these types is extremely cumbersome and I have every intention of taking examples from a whole range of works.

Between the two types of plot occur, with some frequency, transitional elements. Plots are not intrinsically traditional; new variations spring forth spontaneously from time to time. A riddle is a parallelism with the first part of the parallel omitted and with the possibility of several substitutions. Very often riddles have many solutions; one of them, the proper one, is considered genuine. But a riddle is calculated so as to suggest to the reader an improper solution. Here are some examples, taken from a book by D. Sovodnikov, *The Riddles of Russian People.* I'm quoting from memory, but I believe, with absolute accuracy:

> Bend me,
> Break me,
> Climb on me,
> I have [it].

The solution is—a "nut tree."

Another, more simple example is: "What is under a woman's skirt?"

The answer is "a hem."

Now for a giant leap. The fact of the matter is that I have to compare the unknown with the known—the structure of a literary work with the structure of a film, which makes two unknowns, since virtually nothing has been done in the theory of literature, either.

Guy de Maupassant, Turgenev, Tolstoy all used parallelism extensively. Nearly every novella of Guy de Maupassant is broken into two components, connected by the unity of the narrator; thus parallels result.

Take the story of a dog that, though utterly devoted to his master, is given as a present to someone else, and the story of a woman whom the same person has married off to a farmer. The story of love among the birds, compared to the story of human love.

In Turgenev, parallelism is obtained chiefly by pursuing the theme of nature throughout the book.

Tolstoy draws a parallel between two human destinies ("Two Hussars"); or between the destiny of a man and that of a horse ("Kholstomer"); or he juxtaposes one group of people against another (*War and Peace, Anna Karenina*). The connection between the parts of the parallel is almost always absolutely formal.

Another line of plot development derives from the riddle. Here we encounter Anne Radcliffe, Walter Scott, Edgar Allan Poe, Balzac, Dostoevsky, Conan Doyle and, strange as it may seem, Pushkin in some of his prose pieces.

In Radcliffe's novels (for example, *The Mysteries of Udolpho*), we are plunged immediately into a mysterious atmosphere.

Letters of mysterious significance, chained-up skeletons, mysterious sighs, apparitions, disappearance and vague hints at the possibility of incest. In Part Two, the mysteries are clarified; their elucidation, however, for the most part, leaves much to be desired and is too far-fetched.

Dickens extensively developed the mystery technique. Let me just list the mysteries of the novel *Little Dorrit.*

This is the order in which they appear. The mystery of the watch belonging to Arthur's father, the mystery of Mrs. Flintwinch's dreams, the mystery of the noises in the house, the mystery of the Dorrit inheritance, the mystery of Rigaud, the mystery of Little Dorrit's love, the Merdle mystery, etc.

Every mystery appears at the appropriate time and occupies several chapters; then it is resolved.

The key mystery—the mystery of Arthur's descent—is revealed only at the very end of the book.

In mystery novels the denouement is usually a failure. Goethe's resolution of his *Wilhelm Meister* is a failure, too. This is why Dickens developed a special device for the denouement of his novels. People get together and tell each other how all the mysteries in the novel got resolved.

Now let's analyze the novel *Our Mutual Friend*. The greatest charm of this work lies in the paradoxical way in which the components of the novel are connected.

Never before had Dickens constructed a more complex edifice. The basic fabula is as follows. A certain miser, Harmon, who has disowned his son, dies.

He leaves a will according to which all his property goes to the disinherited son, on condition that he marry a certain young girl with whom the heir himself is barely acquainted.

He had seen her once as a little girl.

Before John Harmon goes to collect his inheritance, he decides that he will put his fiancée to the test. She passes with flying colors, so he reveals to her his true name. Now let's see how this fabula is elaborated into a plot.

The whole secret of the novel, as Dickens himself explains in the afterword, lies in the fact that he had never concealed from the reader that John Rokesmith is none other than John Harmon. Though not concealing this fact, Dickens nonetheless uses this quasi-mystery to lead the reader astray.

The true mystery of the novel is the fact that Mr. and Mrs.

Boffin both know that they employ the son of their master himself as their secretary.

They are busy mystifying Bella, forcing her to clarify her relationship with John and, at the same time, show her better side. The reader does not solve this rather primitive mystery because he is on the wrong track.

The screen version of *Our Mutual Friend* was not successful. To start with, most of the parallel intrigues in the script had to be scrapped.

The usual connection in a novel—one person related to another—cannot be conveyed on the screen.

The script retained only three story lines: 1) the story of John Harmon and Bella; 2) the story of Eugene and Lizzie; 3) the story of the Wegg plot.

To make matters worse, these lines are not interwoven; they are completely disconnected, because the connecting part is omitted.

In Dickens this part might be called "What the World Thinks." Periodically, Dickens shifts the scene to the Veneering salon, where various events are being discussed. This device is analogous to the device in Tolstoy's *War and Peace.* The Dickensian double mystery device (one real, the other false) was a total flop; the authors of adaptation hardly even suspected its existence.

Parallel intrigues in a film are possible only on one condition: that they be connected by common characters.

Everything that goes by the name of Dickensian humor—that is, the idiosyncratic structure of the language, the unique use of words, irony—did not work on the screen.

The people turned out to be the same as they were in real life, and not "as they were written in the novel." Things remain "unperturbed."

Actually, film uses both "mystery" and "parallel" extensively, but it uses them in its own way.

Mystery is used in the cinema mainly for plot transpositions.

Plot transposition is the phenomenon whereby a work's events are rendered not in sequence, but in some other order.

Usually what motivates the transposition is a story.

Thus in Pushkin's "Shot" we first see Silvio at target practice with his revolver. It is only later that we find out about his unfinished duel with the count.

By means of such motivation Gogol provides the genesis of Chichikov; John Harmon of Dickens's *Our Mutual*

Friend tells himself a story about the error of his death (a friend with whom he had traded clothes is killed).

The same device is found in Walter Scott, in Dostoevsky's *Raw Youth,* etc.

The detective novel has triumphed over the robber novel, because the robber novel derives from the adventure novel, where the impeded actions are accomplished by a mere accumulation of obstacles on the hero's path, whereas the detective novel offers the possibility of a brand-new construct. At first, we see a mystery-crime, then we're provided with possibilities for its resolution and, finally, we have the whole picture.

Thus the "detective novel" is nothing but a mystery novel with a professional sleuth. In film, plot displacement triumphs. First, we usually get several somewhat incomprehensible scenes, which are explained only later in the form of a story narrated by one of the characters. Note, however, that in the case of motivation by a story, it is not the story of an event, as in a novel, but a plot transposition in its purest form (i.e., it's as if you snipped a piece of film off the beginning and put it at the end).

In that regard film is undoubtedly much stronger. It is much weaker, however, in the area of allusion, which in literature sustains one's interest in the resolution of mystery. Film does not allow ambivalence.

Parallelism of action in a novel has been frequently used for yet another purpose—to impede the action.

In those cases the hero or heroine of one component in the parallel construct is abandoned at the moment of crisis and the action shifts to another parallel. Thus in *The Brothers Karamzov,* Books 6 and 7 cut into the most highly charged moment (the moment of the preparations for the murder of Fyodor Pavlovich).

In *Crime and Punishment,* too, the two themes—Raskolnikov's fate and Svidrigailov's fate—interrupt one another.

We see what may be the same technique of two simultaneous intrigues in *King Lear.*

In Hoffman's *The Life and Opinions of Kater Murr*, the biography of Johannes Kreisler is interrupted by the story of the cat. The technique of interruption is interesting in itself. Toward the end of Part 2, everyone expresses surprise at the princess's speedy recovery. The doctor ascribes it to a "violent shock to all the nerves"—the result of a nocturnal walk to the Mary Chapel. The doctor says that he would certainly have known about such a treatment and that he had merely forgotten to recommend strongly such a walk.

However, Benzon thinks to herself: "Hmm—the old woman has been with her."

Now the time has come to clarify this mysterious matter: "(M. c.)—love me, charming Miesmies? Oh, tell me again, tell me a thousand times so that I can go into greater raptures . . . " Another example follows (from Part 4):[11]

> "Child," replied the Meister in his serious manner, "child, something beautiful and wonderful, but its not right that you should learn about it. Let those mechanical things finish their tricks while I confide in you as much as is necessary and useful for you to know. My dear Julia, your own mother has kept her heart locked up from you. I wish to open it for you so that you may look inside and recognize the danger in which you hover and will be able to escape it. First, you must learn without any more digressions, that your mother has decided nothing less than—"

Now Murr enters the picture:

> (M. c.)—rather let it go. Youthful cats, be modest as I am and not always ready with a poem when

---

11 Translations from *Selected Writings of E. T. A. Hoffman,* ed. and trans. Leonard J. Kent and Elizabeth C. Knight.

simple, honest prose will do to spin out your thoughts. Poems should do for prose what lard does for sausage; namely, they should be sprinkled through to give the whole mishmash more glistening fat, more sweetness of taste.

Here is what motivates the interruption (Editor's Preface):

The printing began, and the first proofs came to the editor's view. How alarmed he was when he noticed that Murr's story breaks off now and then and that strange interpolations occur which belong to another book containing the biography of Kappellmesiter Johannes Kresiler.

After careful investigation and inquiry, the editor finally learned the following. When Kater Murr wrote his life and opinions, he unceremoniously ripped up a printed book which he found at his master's and simply used the leaves, partly as an underpad, partly as blotting paper. These papers remained in the manuscript and, by mistake, were printed as if they belonged to it.

"Braking" in a novel, the postponement of plot resolution, is very often attained by the use of material that is extraneous to the plot, rather than by a shift to a parallel theme at the critical moment. Radcliffe does it by sentimental descriptions, Dostoevsky by the speeches of the characters on various philosophical themes. Dostoevsky himself sometimes underscored the literary nature of those interpolations, their unusual length.

Here is a conversation between Raskolnikov and Svidrigailov; it has been going on for ten pages already (Part IV, Chapter 1).

These two people see each other for the first time in their lives:

> "I don't believe in a future life," said Raskonikov. Svidrigailov sat pondering. "—What if there are only spiders there or something of the sort?" he said suddenly. "This is a madman," thought Raskolnikov.
>
> "We always imagine eternity as an idea that is impossible to comprehend, as something immense, immense. Why necessarily immense? Imagine that, all of a sudden, instead of all of this, it turns out to be one little room, like a village bathhouse, with soot and spiders in every corner—and that's

all of eternity for you. You know, I sometimes have visions of this sort."

"Don't you ever envision anything more soothing and more just?" exclaimed Raskolnikov with alarm.

"More just. Well, how do we know? Perhaps this is just, and, mind you, I would have arranged it in precisely the same way," said Svidrigailov, with a vague smile.

Having heard this repulsive reply, Raskolnikov was suddenly seized by a sort of chill. Svidrigailov lifted his head, looked at him intently and burst out laughing.

"Oh, no, just think about it!" he shrieked. "Half an hour ago, we hadn't even seen each other yet; we are regarded as enemies. We still had that affair of ours to settle, yet we have abandoned all that business and ventured into such literature."

Sometimes the discourse of Dostoevsky's heroes sound like true "literature" or even journalism. This is taken, once again, from one of Svidrigailov's conversations (Part VI, Chapter 3):

"Oh, yes, there's more: I'm convinced that there are many people in Petersburg who wander around talking to themselves. This is a city of crazy people. If we had had the sciences, then doctors, lawyers and philosophers all could have carried out the most valuable studies, each in his own field. It is rare to find a place other than Petersburg where so many somber, radical and strange influences are exerted on the human soul. As if the climate alone weren't enough! And yet, this is the administrative center of all of Russia, and its character must be reflected in everything . . ."

In a film, one action interrupts another in perfect canonic fashion. However, a film interruption differs in its structure from the interruption in a novel. In novels, one plot element is interrupted by another. We are dealing with the alternation of situations. In a film, those segments which interrupt one another are much shorter; they are truly segments; we usually return to the same moment of the action. The most typical interruption in a film is a kind of "prolonged rescue." The hero or heroine is being killed. "Meanwhile" we see that the victim's friends are either unaware of her plight or unable to help her, etc. Then once again someone perishes before our eyes, etc.

A certain man of letters, an acquaintance of mine, once pointed out to me that attempted rape in a modern film is almost canonized. The victim is struggling, her friends are far away, the villain is pursuing the woman, "meanwhile," etc. In my opinion, the choice of the crime in this instance is explained not so much by the desire to play on the spectator's interest in eroticism as by the actual nature of the crime, which requires for its completion a certain amount of time. Instead of rape, take murder by pistol shot. Such an act is too indivisible. That is why cinematic villainy is usually perpetrated by a method that requires a large amount of time—drowning, for example, with the victim suspended upside down in a cellar and water pouring in. Sometimes the victim is bound hand and foot, then tossed on the railroad tracks, or else immured. Also effective is abduction in all its varieties. Only minor characters, not involved in the plot, are killed off immediately. Also utilized is the elaboration, or rather the extension, of the action by means of landscapes, which function as a braking factor or a parallel.

One curious trait of cinematography is its complete disregard of motivations. By "motivations" I mean the common, "quotidian" (or *bytovoe*)[12] explanation of a plot structure. In a broader sense, our (morphological) school considers each and every kind of semantic justification for an artistic structure as its "motivation." Motivation in an artistic structure is a secondary phenomenon.

Edgar Allan Poe's story about how "The Raven" was written is, for the most part, a description of how he constructed the motivation for the artistic form. Motivation is used extensively in European art, even in fantasy fiction. Sorcery and magic are motivations of a sort, too. E. T. A. Hoffmann's stories often contain within themselves the possibility of explaining the fantastic by the real. Film has almost no use for motivations. Maybe this is simplistic, but it seems to me that in film nothing is told; everything is shown.

We don't require detailed explanations of the exceptionally fortuitous turn of events that made possible someone's rescue. The facts speak for themselves. We see a film and hardly ever ask ourselves "how, in what way?" An ordinary contemporary stunt film consists of a number of engaging

12 The Russian word "быт" has no English equivalent. The adjective derived from it, "bytovoe," means "pertaining to everyday life"; it incorporates the shades of meaning "common," "trivial," "prosaic."

scenes which are connected with each other solely by the unity of the characters.

Nor is any psychological motivation supplied. One part of a film is indispensable, because in it the cameraman shows a view of a city from above; in the next part, a trained monkey performs; the third part of the same film contains a ballet performance, and so on. And we watch all of it with interest. What is a film plot? An artful selection of scenes, a successful chronological transposition and good juxtapositions.

The film script has turned both toward popular comedy, with its stock characters, and toward the adventure novel, with its highly developed use of "delaying elements," with its wide range of casualties, drownings, desert islands and other tricks, which resemble, above all, the devices of the Greek adventure novel. I do not consider it superfluous to mention that A. I. Veselovsky considers all the "delaying elements" in the Greek novel not as a reproduction of the peculiarities of Greek life, but as distinctive stylistic devices.[13]

The "delaying elements," braking the development of the

13 *Беллетристика у древникх греков* (Belles-letters of Ancient Greeks) (Vestnik Europi, 1876), p. 683.

action and creating impediments in the plot, are essential to the creation of an "aesthetic" experience with marked tension, both in the adventure novel and in the motion picture; their role is similar to that of parallelisms, sound orchestration, etc., in a poem.

Since "delaying elements," with slight variations, can go on forever, the only way to end the screenplay is to have a wedding (i.e., a love story is used to create a frame novella).

Since the cinema relies on combinations of plot motifs, and not on the exposition of characters, the motion picture developed something akin to Italian comedy—masks, as they were called; that is, stock characters. Hence these stock characters in cinematography who proceed from one film to another without even changing their makeup, let alone their names: such are Glupyshkin (forgotten already), Max Linder, Paxon, and the famous Charlie Chaplin and his troupe. Charlie Chaplin requires a detailed examination.

Chaplin has played innumerable parts—Chaplin the soldier, Chaplin at the bank, Chaplin the policeman, Chaplin the patient at the spa, and even Chaplin the movie actor. This may be a manifestation of the need to create disparities, which compels a fiction writer to turn one of his images into a permanent paragon (a yardstick for comparison) for the entire work of art.

Through Chaplin the spectator tries out various professions; he tests them and, in the process, discards them. Chaplin is undoubtedly the most cinematic actor of all. His scripts are not written: they are created during the shooting. He is nearly the only movie actor who originates from the material itself.

Chaplin's gestures and films are conceived not in the word, nor in the drawing, but in the flicker of the gray-and-black shadow. Chaplin has broken with the theater once and for all, so, of course, he deserves the title—the first movie actor.

It must be noted that Chaplin never speaks in a film, and no explanatory subtitles appear on the screen between the separate components of his films. Some Russian movie actors told me that, in order to connect the several elements of the cinematic poses with an emotion, they have to whisper various appropriate phrases. This is noticeable if you look at the actor's lips as the plot proceeds. In his films, Chaplin doesn't speak—he moves. He works with the cinematic material instead of translating himself from theatrical into screen language. I cannot define right now what makes Chaplin's movement comical—perhaps the fact that it is mechanized.

Chaplin's acting can be divided into a number of passages, each of them ending with a period-pose.

If we resort to metaphor, we can say that Chaplin's movement is like a dotted line. Apparently, Chaplin himself is aware of all the dance steps in his art. His acting can be broken into a number of "constant movements" that are repeated in various films, but with different motivations. Here are some of them: Chaplin walking (the very moment of take-off evokes laughter), Chaplin on the stairs, Chaplin touching someone with the hook of his cane, Chaplin falling off a chair (bow-legged, frozen in this position for a minute), Chaplin smiling (three beats), Chaplin being seized by the collar and shaken, etc. I don't know whether it's intentional but Chaplin's ensemble moves differently than its leader. At this point an interesting question arises: is Chaplin's motion comical in and of itself or is it comical as a contrast to normal motion (in cinematic transmission)?

I am curious to see how Chaplin bares the purely cinematic essence of all the constituents in his films, such as *Chaplin at the Movies* and *Chaplin and Anna B.*: the trick is out in the open. To clarify my idea, I'll translate it into literary material.

Ostrovsky wrote a whole series of plays containing both a tragic figure and a comic figure. Each time both of these types would have a motivation based on everyday life (for instance, the tragic figure is Lyubim the woodcutter, the comic figure is a bureaucrat). But then Ostrovksy wrote *The Forest.* The tragic figure in that play is tragic; the comic figure is comic. The mask is presented without the social motivation. Chaplin has once again demonstrated all the stunts of cinematography—falling down a manhole, knocking down objects, being kicked in the rear—and this is all palatable. We can eat it hot. But I'm interested in knowing where Chaplin goes from here. It seems to me that the film *Chaplin at the Movies* betrays a certain weariness of the stunt. History shows that, as forms develop, both the baring of the device and the parody of a phenomenon signal the end of a given cycle.

I suspect that Chaplin will now gravitate towards films which combine comedy with heroic elements (i.e., he will make use of comedy combined with suspense).

Unfortunately I do not know the chronology of Chaplin's films, but if *Chaplin and the Salvation Army* is one of his latest, then he may have already started down this path.

The Future of the Motion Picture

And what path will the motion picture choose?

I think several. Fortunately, art always subdivides into several tendencies, with one prevailing over the rest, which are held in reserve. Sure to succeed is the thriller, with its chase scenes that have become canonical in cinematography, to say nothing of its murders, both successful and unsuccessful, and its chronological transpositions.

One separate branch of the thriller that is sure to develop is the American film geared toward special effects, with acrobatic numbers and minimal focus on acting, but with lots of animals, train wrecks, etc., used as material for the artistic structure.

Such films will be more interesting by virtue of their material. The motivation in them will deteriorate more and more. The end result will be some sort of variety show. Let's hope the psychological, high-society film, whose action takes place in a drawing room, becomes extinct. This type of film is a relic of the theater. What keeps it going is the fact that, although the uptown crowd doesn't care much for the theater, it respects this kind of film and, out of respect, is willing to spend ten minutes watching a simulacrum of the theater.

Here we see the desire to be cultured. As for the costumed historical epic film, its future is not quite clear. At present, these films are popular. This is not too surprising, since film, lacking the capacity to transmit a separate continuous movement, has no difficulty handling mass movement. But such films have great limitations; lush costumes and customs are not inexhaustible.

The success of Chaplin-type films is undeniable. In all likelihood, classical cinematography will grow out of them. There is yet one other line along which cinematography may evolve. It is the animated film. After seeing them several times, I am convinced that they have possibilities that are, as yet, untapped. What is interesting about them is the awareness of the toy-like nature of the moving character. The sense of the illusory is a very important element in the old theater, and it has been used artfully, sometimes suppressed, sometimes rediscovered. The motion picture is, of course, very conventional, as conventional as photography itself, but we have trained ourselves to perceive the world through a photograph, so the conventionality of the cinema is hardly noticed.

Thus one of the options for an artistic structure, the game of illusion, is vanishing. Maybe cartoons can be combined with regular films? In any case, what is meant to happen will happen.

They say about Russian literature that it is the most moral literature in the world. That is a poor recommendation for literary morality. They also say that Russian literature is filled with love for one's neighbor. This tradition compels me to raise in this article on literature and cinematography the issue of morality and cinematography. Is cinematography ruining people's morals? They say that literature improves them. Literary morality is, of course, not the morality of those who write literature; otherwise, I might have referred to the outrageous biography of Krylov. By the way, no one is familiar with it.

It is unlikely, however, that morality is inherent in literature. "Yesterday there was a big fire," wrote the old Lev Tolstoy in his diary; "the tailor and his entire family burned to death. Too bad I didn't go have a look."

Fire, hunger, grief—these are all material for literature.

Without attempting to resolve this controversial issue, I will say one thing. Whatever else it may do, an adventure novel usually depicts actions which are basically virtuous.

Even if art had the obligation to summon people to do noble deeds, the adventure film would still have a higher place than the "confession of Nikolai Stavrogin." But I, personally, am inclined to think that works of art are never either moral or immoral. Remember the cruelty we find in fairy tales, and yet children all over the world tell them.

Tumbling down a ravine in a barrel studded with nails is not horrifying in a fairy tale. That is not cruelty, but art. The blood in art is not bloody. Nor, unfortunately, is the nobility in art true to life. The French terrorists are sentimental people.

Art takes everything as its material. Remember that the spring dancing song is about death and a jealous, pugnacious husband.[14] This is tragic, but it is tragedy in a song. Art is not an inscription, but an ornament. Lev Tolstoy was absolutely correct when he said that you have to have the same fondness for novels that you have for tumbler-pigeons.

Since art flows like a river and since it is made like the weather, without asking anyone's advice, then all we can do is take note of the facts.

---

14 *The Rites of Spring Song.*

As to the effect that film has on literature, it may be of a dual nature.

At first, literature seizes upon cinematic devices and imitates them. Maybe some other phenomenon, more serious, will come along. Maybe literature will move into a purely linguistic sphere and relinquish plot.

Something like that happened with the advent of photography: photography took away the taste for naturalism.

Acknowledgments

I wish to express deep gratitude to my mentor, professor Wallace Martin, who has been the engine that propelled this book forward. Wally inspired me to start this translation and, more importantly, helped me sustain the momentum necessary for its completion. Our shared love for Viktor Shklovsky is the foundation of our mutual desire to expand the audience of the writer's fans. It is about broadcasting the knowledge of the extraordinary vision Shklovsky possessed, not only as a literary critic and the father of Russian formalism, but as a human being with a gift for connecting the particular with the universal.

—Rina Masinovsky

SELECTED DALKEY ARCHIVE PAPERBACKS

PETROS ABATZOGLOU, *What Does Mrs. Freeman Want?*
PIERRE ALBERT-BIROT, *Grabinoulor.*
YUZ ALESHKOVSKY, *Kangaroo.*
FELIPE ALFAU, *Chromos.*
　　Locos.
IVAN ÂNGELO, *The Celebration.*
　　The Tower of Glass.
DAVID ANTIN, *Talking.*
ANTÓNIO LOBO ANTUNES, *Knowledge of Hell.*
ALAIN ARIAS-MISSON, *Theatre of Incest.*
DJUNA BARNES, *Ladies Almanack.*
　　Ryder.
JOHN BARTH, *LETTERS.*
　　Sabbatical.
DONALD BARTHELME, *The King.*
　　Paradise.
SVETISLAV BASARA, *Chinese Letter.*
MARK BINELLI, *Sacco and Vanzetti Must Die!*
ANDREI BITOV, *Pushkin House.*
LOUIS PAUL BOON, *Chapel Road.*
　　Summer in Termuren.
ROGER BOYLAN, *Killoyle.*
IGNÁCIO DE LOYOLA BRANDÃO, *Teeth under the Sun.*
　　Zero.
BONNIE BREMSER, *Troia: Mexican Memoirs.*
CHRISTINE BROOKE-ROSE, *Amalgamemnon.*
BRIGID BROPHY, *In Transit.*
MEREDITH BROSNAN, *Mr. Dynamite.*
GERALD L. BRUNS,
　　Modern Poetry and the Idea of Language.
EVGENY BUNIMOVICH AND J. KATES, EDS.,
　　Contemporary Russian Poetry: An Anthology.
GABRIELLE BURTON, *Heartbreak Hotel.*
MICHEL BUTOR, *Degrees.*
　　Mobile.
　　Portrait of the Artist as a Young Ape.
G. CABRERA INFANTE, *Infante's Inferno.*
　　Three Trapped Tigers.
JULIETA CAMPOS, *The Fear of Losing Eurydice.*
ANNE CARSON, *Eros the Bittersweet.*
CAMILO JOSÉ CELA, *Christ versus Arizona.*
　　The Family of Pascual Duarte.
　　The Hive.
LOUIS-FERDINAND CÉLINE, *Castle to Castle.*
　　Conversations with Professor Y.
　　London Bridge.
　　North.
　　Rigadoon.
HUGO CHARTERIS, *The Tide Is Right.*
JEROME CHARYN, *The Tar Baby.*
MARC CHOLODENKO, *Mordechai Schamz.*
EMILY HOLMES COLEMAN, *The Shutter of Snow.*
ROBERT COOVER, *A Night at the Movies.*
STANLEY CRAWFORD, *Some Instructions to My Wife.*
ROBERT CREELEY, *Collected Prose.*
RENÉ CREVEL, *Putting My Foot in It.*
RALPH CUSACK, *Cadenza.*
SUSAN DAITCH, *L.C.*
　　Storytown.
NICHOLAS DELBANCO, *The Count of Concord.*
NIGEL DENNIS, *Cards of Identity.*
PETER DIMOCK,
　　A Short Rhetoric for Leaving the Family.
ARIEL DORFMAN, *Konfidenz.*
COLEMAN DOWELL, *The Houses of Children.*
　　Island People.
　　Too Much Flesh and Jabez.
RIKKI DUCORNET, *The Complete Butcher's Tales.*
　　The Fountains of Neptune.
　　The Jade Cabinet.
　　Phosphor in Dreamland.
　　The Stain.
　　The Word "Desire."
WILLIAM EASTLAKE, *The Bamboo Bed.*
　　Castle Keep.
　　Lyric of the Circle Heart.
JEAN ECHENOZ, *Chopin's Move.*
STANLEY ELKIN, *A Bad Man.*
　　Boswell: A Modern Comedy.
　　Criers and Kibitzers, Kibitzers and Criers.
　　The Dick Gibson Show.
　　The Franchiser.
　　George Mills.
　　The Living End.
　　The MacGuffin.
　　The Magic Kingdom.
　　Mrs. Ted Bliss.
　　The Rabbi of Lud.
　　Van Gogh's Room at Arles.

ANNIE ERNAUX, *Cleaned Out.*
LAUREN FAIRBANKS, *Muzzle Thyself.*
　　Sister Carrie.
LESLIE A. FIEDLER,
　　Love and Death in the American Novel.
GUSTAVE FLAUBERT, *Bouvard and Pécuchet.*
FORD MADOX FORD, *The March of Literature.*
JON FOSSE, *Melancholy.*
MAX FRISCH, *I'm Not Stiller.*
　　Man in the Holocene.
CARLOS FUENTES, *Christopher Unborn.*
　　Distant Relations.
　　Terra Nostra.
　　Where the Air Is Clear.
JANICE GALLOWAY, *Foreign Parts.*
　　The Trick Is to Keep Breathing.
WILLIAM H. GASS, *A Temple of Texts.*
　　The Tunnel.
　　Willie Masters' Lonesome Wife.
ETIENNE GILSON, *The Arts of the Beautiful.*
　　Forms and Substances in the Arts.
C. S. GISCOMBE, *Giscome Road.*
　　Here.
DOUGLAS GLOVER, *Bad News of the Heart.*
　　The Enamoured Knight.
WITOLD GOMBROWICZ, *A Kind of Testament.*
KAREN ELIZABETH GORDON, *The Red Shoes.*
GEORGI GOSPODINOV, *Natural Novel.*
JUAN GOYTISOLO, *Count Julian.*
　　Makbara.
　　Marks of Identity.
PATRICK GRAINVILLE, *The Cave of Heaven.*
HENRY GREEN, *Blindness.*
　　Concluding.
　　Doting.
　　Nothing.
JIŘÍ GRUŠA, *The Questionnaire.*
GABRIEL GUDDING, *Rhode Island Notebook.*
JOHN HAWKES, *Whistlejacket.*
AIDAN HIGGINS, *A Bestiary.*
　　Bornholm Night-Ferry.
　　Flotsam and Jetsam.
　　Langrishe, Go Down.
　　Scenes from a Receding Past.
　　Windy Arbours.
ALDOUS HUXLEY, *Antic Hay.*
　　Crome Yellow.
　　Point Counter Point.
　　Those Barren Leaves.
　　Time Must Have a Stop.
MIKHAIL IOSSEL AND JEFF PARKER, EDS., *Amerika:*
　　Contemporary Russians View the United States.
GERT JONKE, *Geometric Regional Novel.*
JACQUES JOUET, *Mountain R.*
HUGH KENNER, *The Counterfeiters.*
　　Flaubert, Joyce and Beckett:
　　The Stoic Comedians.
　　Joyce's Voices.
DANILO KIŠ, *Garden, Ashes.*
　　A Tomb for Boris Davidovich.
ANITA KONKKA, *A Fool's Paradise.*
GEORGE KONRÁD, *The City Builder.*
TADEUSZ KONWICKI, *A Minor Apocalypse.*
　　The Polish Complex.
MENIS KOUMANDAREAS, *Koula.*
ELAINE KRAF, *The Princess of 72nd Street.*
JIM KRUSOE, *Iceland.*
EWA KURYLUK, *Century 21.*
VIOLETTE LEDUC, *La Bâtarde.*
DEBORAH LEVY, *Billy and Girl.*
　　Pillow Talk in Europe and Other Places.
JOSÉ LEZAMA LIMA, *Paradiso.*
ROSA LIKSOM, *Dark Paradise.*
OSMAN LINS, *Avalovara.*
　　The Queen of the Prisons of Greece.
ALF MAC LOCHLAINN, *The Corpus in the Library.*
　　Out of Focus.
RON LOEWINSOHN, *Magnetic Field(s).*
D. KEITH MANO, *Take Five.*
BEN MARCUS, *The Age of Wire and String.*
WALLACE MARKFIELD, *Teitlebaum's Window.*
　　To an Early Grave.
DAVID MARKSON, *Reader's Block.*
　　Springer's Progress.
　　Wittgenstein's Mistress.
CAROLE MASO, *AVA.*
LADISLAV MATEJKA AND KRYSTYNA POMORSKA, EDS.,
　　Readings in Russian Poetics: Formalist and
　　Structuralist Views.

FOR A FULL LIST OF PUBLICATIONS, VISIT:
www.dalkeyarchive.com

HARRY MATHEWS,
  The Case of the Persevering Maltese: Collected Essays.
  Cigarettes.
  The Conversions.
  The Human Country: New and Collected Stories.
  The Journalist.
  My Life in CIA.
  Singular Pleasures.
  The Sinking of the Odradek Stadium.
  Tlooth.
  20 Lines a Day.
ROBERT L. McLAUGHLIN, ED.,
  Innovations: An Anthology of Modern &
    Contemporary Fiction.
HERMAN MELVILLE, *The Confidence-Man.*
AMANDA MICHALOPOULOU, *I'd Like.*
STEVEN MILLHAUSER, *The Barnum Museum.*
  In the Penny Arcade.
RALPH J. MILLS, JR., *Essays on Poetry.*
OLIVE MOORE, *Spleen.*
NICHOLAS MOSLEY, *Accident.*
  Assassins.
  Catastrophe Practice.
  Children of Darkness and Light.
  Experience and Religion.
  The Hesperides Tree.
  Hopeful Monsters.
  Imago Bird.
  Impossible Object.
  Inventing God.
  Judith.
  Look at the Dark.
  Natalie Natalia.
  Serpent.
  Time at War.
  The Uses of Slime Mould: Essays of Four Decades.
WARREN F. MOTTE, JR.,
  Fables of the Novel: French Fiction since 1990.
  Fiction Now: The French Novel in the 21st Century.
  Oulipo: A Primer of Potential Literature.
YVES NAVARRE, *Our Share of Time.*
  Sweet Tooth.
DOROTHY NELSON, *In Night's City.*
  Tar and Feathers.
WILFRIDO D. NOLLEDO, *But for the Lovers.*
FLANN O'BRIEN, *At Swim-Two-Birds.*
  At War.
  The Best of Myles.
  The Dalkey Archive.
  Further Cuttings.
  The Hard Life.
  The Poor Mouth.
  The Third Policeman.
CLAUDE OLLIER, *The Mise-en-Scène.*
PATRIK OUŘEDNÍK, *Europeana.*
FERNANDO DEL PASO, *Palinuro of Mexico.*
ROBERT PINGET, *The Inquisitory.*
  Mahu or The Material.
  Trio.
RAYMOND QUENEAU, *The Last Days.*
  Odile.
  Pierrot Mon Ami.
  Saint Glinglin.
ANN QUIN, *Berg.*
  Passages.
  Three.
  Tripticks.
ISHMAEL REED, *The Free-Lance Pallbearers.*
  The Last Days of Louisiana Red.
  Reckless Eyeballing.
  The Terrible Threes.
  The Terrible Twos.
  Yellow Back Radio Broke-Down.
JEAN RICARDOU, *Place Names.*
JULIÁN RÍOS, *Larva: A Midsummer Night's Babel.*
  Poundemonium.
AUGUSTO ROA BASTOS, *I the Supreme.*
OLIVIER ROLIN, *Hotel Crystal.*
JACQUES ROUBAUD, *The Great Fire of London.*
  Hortense in Exile.
  Hortense Is Abducted.
  The Plurality of Worlds of Lewis.
  The Princess Hoppy.
  The Form of a City Changes Faster, Alas,
    Than the Human Heart.

Some Thing Black.
LEON S. ROUDIEZ, *French Fiction Revisited.*
VEDRANA RUDAN, *Night.*
LYDIE SALVAYRE, *The Company of Ghosts.*
  Everyday Life.
  The Lecture.
  The Power of Flies.
LUIS RAFAEL SÁNCHEZ, *Macho Camacho's Beat.*
SEVERO SARDUY, *Cobra & Maitreya.*
NATHALIE SARRAUTE, *Do You Hear Them?*
  Martereau.
  The Planetarium.
ARNO SCHMIDT, *Collected Stories.*
  Nobodaddy's Children.
CHRISTINE SCHUTT, *Nightwork.*
GAIL SCOTT, *My Paris.*
JUNE AKERS SEESE,
  Is This What Other Women Feel Too?
  What Waiting Really Means.
AURELIE SHEEHAN, *Jack Kerouac Is Pregnant.*
VIKTOR SHKLOVSKY, *Knight's Move.*
  A Sentimental Journey: Memoirs 1917-1922.
  Energy of Delusion: A Book on Plot.
  Literature and Cinematography.
  Theory of Prose.
  Third Factory.
  Zoo, or Letters Not about Love.
JOSEF ŠKVORECKÝ,
  The Engineer of Human Souls.
CLAUDE SIMON, *The Invitation.*
GILBERT SORRENTINO, *Aberration of Starlight.*
  Blue Pastoral.
  Crystal Vision.
  Imaginative Qualities of Actual Things.
  Mulligan Stew.
  Pack of Lies.
  Red the Fiend.
  The Sky Changes.
  Something Said.
  Splendide-Hôtel.
  Steelwork.
  Under the Shadow.
W. M. SPACKMAN, *The Complete Fiction.*
GERTRUDE STEIN, *Lucy Church Amiably.*
  The Making of Americans.
  A Novel of Thank You.
PIOTR SZEWC, *Annihilation.*
STEFAN THEMERSON, *Hobson's Island.*
  The Mystery of the Sardine.
  Tom Harris.
JEAN-PHILIPPE TOUSSAINT, *Monsieur.*
  Television.
DUMITRU TSEPENEAG, *Vain Art of the Fugue.*
ESTHER TUSQUETS, *Stranded.*
DUBRAVKA UGRESIC, *Lend Me Your Character.*
  Thank You for Not Reading.
MATI UNT, *Diary of a Blood Donor.*
  Things in the Night.
ELOY URROZ, *The Obstacles.*
LUISA VALENZUELA, *He Who Searches.*
PAUL VERHAEGHEN, *Omega Minor.*
MARJA-LIISA VARTIO, *The Parson's Widow.*
BORIS VIAN, *Heartsnatcher.*
AUSTRYN WAINHOUSE, *Hedyphagetica.*
PAUL WEST, *Words for a Deaf Daughter & Gala.*
CURTIS WHITE, *America's Magic Mountain.*
  The Idea of Home.
  Memories of My Father Watching TV.
  Monstrous Possibility: An Invitation to
    Literary Politics.
  Requiem.
DIANE WILLIAMS, *Excitability: Selected Stories.*
  Romancer Erector.
DOUGLAS WOOLF, *Wall to Wall.*
  Ya! & John-Juan.
JAY WRIGHT, *Polynomials and Pollen.*
  The Presentable Art of Reading Absence.
PHILIP WYLIE, *Generation of Vipers.*
MARGUERITE YOUNG, *Angel in the Forest.*
  Miss MacIntosh, My Darling.
REYOUNG, *Unbabbling.*
ZORAN ŽIVKOVIĆ, *Hidden Camera.*
LOUIS ZUKOFSKY, *Collected Fiction.*
SCOTT ZWIREN, *God Head.*
